Contents

1.	What about working in architecture?	1
2.	What sorts of jobs are there?	5
3.	What qualifications will I need?	10
4.	What personal skills and attitudes are needed?	14
5.	How competitive an area is it?	18
6.	What are the good and bad aspects of the work?	19
7.	Where will I work?	20
8.	Who will I work with?	23
9.	What will I earn?	25
10.	What are the hours and holidays like?	27
11.	Will I meet the public?	28
12.	Are the prospects good for my career?	29
13.	What about training at work?	30
14.	Will I need other languages for the work?	31
15.	Will I be able to work overseas or travel for my job?	32
16.	What are the recent developments in this area?	33
17.	What impact has new technology had on this work?	36
18.	Could I become famous?	37
19.	Could I work independently?	38
20.	How can I find out more about the work?	39
21.	What should I do now to prepare?	42
22.	What courses and qualifications are available?	45
23.	What publications should I look at?	46
24.	Which addresses will help me?	48

Q&A

More Questions & Answers available from Trotman

Questions & Answers Careers Series

Accountancy	Law
Advertising	Library & Information Work
Animals	Marketing
Architecture	Medicine
Armed Forces	Modelling
Art & Design	Music
Banking	Nursing
Childcare	Office & Secretarial Work
Complementary Medicine	Photography
Computing	Physiotherapy
Dentistry	Police
Engineering	Psychology
Environment & Conservation	Public Relations
Fashion & Clothing Design	Radio, TV & Film
Fire Service	Retail
Hairdressing	Science
Hotels & Catering	Social Work
Journalism	Sport
Languages	Teaching

Questions & Answers Degree Subject Guides

Studying Art & Design	Studying Drama
Studying Business & Management	Studying English
	Studying Law
Studying Chemical Engineering	Studying Media
	Studying Psychology
Studying Computer Science	Studying Sports Science

Careers in Architecture

your questions and answers

edited by

Tom Lee

TROTMAN

This second edition published in 2002 in Great Britain by Trotman and Company Limited, 2 The Green, Richmond, Surrey TW9 1PL

© Trotman and Company Limited 2002

British Library Cataloguing in Publication Data

A catalogue record for this book is available from the British Library

ISBN 0 85660 768 1

Typeset by Palimpsest Book Production Limited, Polmont, Stirlingshire

Printed and bound in Great Britain by Bell & Bain (Scotland) Ltd

What about working in architecture?

'An art for all to learn because all are concerned with it.'

John Ruskin

Look around you: the fact is that no matter where you live or what you do, every human being has a primary requirement for shelter, security and privacy. Architecture is therefore of fundamental importance to us all.

In primitive society the person seeking these requirements was also responsible for providing them – whether by using a natural feature such as a cave, or by using the materials available to construct a basic dwelling such as a mud hut or wigwam. Client, architect and builder were therefore one and the same person.

As society became more complex, there arose the need for more permanent structures. In addition to the basic dwelling there began to emerge the demand for places and structures to accommodate social functions such as worship, entertainment and general meeting and trading places, as well as accommodation for governments and great leaders. It is in these societies – such as Ancient Egypt – that we first see distinct building professions emerge. Skilled craftsmen would have been chosen for the construction of these large civic buildings, and the profession of architect was born.

Today there are literally hundreds of different professions and career opportunities available within the construction industry. These are broadly divisible into three groups: designers, builders and 'others'.

Designers – Among the design professions are architecture, engineering, interior design, landscape architecture and planning. Each design profession is supported by technicians and administrative staff.

Builders – The building profession consists on the one hand of a wide range of management jobs, and on the other of a large number of skilled building trades. It takes over 20 different skilled trades to construct a simple house.

Others – Together, building and design are supported, where necessary, by an almost infinite number of related specialist professions and businesses. Among them are architectural technologists, acoustics specialists, architectural journalists, building materials manufacturers, computer-aided design (CAD) specialists, construction lawyers, land surveyors, lecturers, machinery designers and manufacturers, project management companies, photographers and quantity surveyors.

The role of the architect

The role of the architect is threefold: businessman (liaising with the client), designer (visualising the building in three dimensions and carrying out the detailed design) and manager (co-ordinating the other professionals involved with the project, known collectively as the 'design team'). Architects therefore occupy a central position within the industry as a whole.

An architect's work involves the initial conceptual design of the building, communication of this design to clients, the design team, builders and others, preparation of detailed design drawings for use on site, and the management of the building project from inception through to completion. The nature of the job means that there is tremendous variety in an architect's work – both from project to project, and from day to day within the same project. No two building projects are the same. Each one will present new challenges in terms of balancing the client's requirements and budget with the design concept, embracing site and location characteristics, choice of materials, the requirements of the various regulatory authorities, accommodating the needs of the other design team members – the list is endless! Even if two buildings appear to be identical there will be aspects of each job which will be different: no two sites are ever the same, the requirements of the local planning authorities will vary, and different people/suppliers will be involved for each project, e.g. the steel manufacturer who was used last time might be too far away for this site, or the bricks that were specified previously might no longer be available.

Architectural projects can last for anything from a few months for a small domestic conversion or extension up to 10–15 years or even longer for a large housing scheme or civic building such as a hospital or concert hall. Large projects can often involve hundreds of design professionals including a team of architects, each one handling a different aspect of the overall design. On smaller projects, however, the architect might be required also to play the part of interior designer, landscape architect, quantity surveyor and structural engineer!

Not all the work an architect does need necessarily be for 'live' projects (i.e. those which are definitely going to be built). Architects are often asked to prepare feasibility studies in which case a report, usually accompanied by drawings and photographs, will be prepared and presented, after which the client might decide not to go ahead. Much time can also be spent by aspiring young architectural practices preparing drawings for architectural competitions, simply to gain the prestige of winning.

If you are creative, good at both arts and sciences, and interested in the built environment, then architecture could well be the career for you. Seeing your thoughts and ideas being converted into buildings which people will use and enjoy for years to come brings a real sense of achievement and satisfaction.

Planning applications

Nearly all architectural projects in the UK will require planning permission from the local authority within whose boundaries the site lies. This applies to building alterations, extensions, road alterations and changes of use for existing properties as well as to new buildings. Planning applications are prepared by the architect and include drawings, site photographs and models to show the site as it is, and the new building(s) as they will look. These are submitted to the local authority together with the appropriate forms and fee for approval.

As part of this procedure, the architect's drawings must be made available for public inspection. If there are any objections raised to the proposals – perhaps by a member of the public – the architect might be asked to argue a case for the scheme during a council meeting.

Building Regulations

The second official set of drawings which has to be prepared by the architect is for Building Regulations approval. The Building Regulations are a set of documents published by the government designed to ensure that all construction work within the UK is carried out to certain standards. Different sections cover specific issues such as structure, heating, insulation, drainage and access for the disabled.

Listed Building Consent

English Heritage has the task of identifying and protecting England's architectural heritage. They do this via a system of listing i.e. recommending buildings for inclusion on statutory lists of buildings of 'special architectural or historic interest' compiled by the Secretary of State for Culture, Media and Sport.

If a client wants to demolish a listed building, or to alter or extend one in any way that affects its character, the architect must obtain 'listed building consent' from the local planning authority.

What sorts of jobs are there?

In addition to architects and their immediate support staff, there is an almost infinite number of specialist careers within the wider architectural profession, making it accessible to people with a broad range of qualifications, talents and abilities. Among these are architectural historians, architectural journalists, construction lawyers, architectural technologists, interior designers, landscape architects, lecturers, lighting or acoustics engineers, model-makers, perspective artists and photographers.

However, the number of different careers actually represented within a typical architects' office is quite small: usually including only architects, architectural technologists and support staff (secretaries, accountants, etc).

Architect

The term 'architect' is a generic term like 'doctor' or 'lawyer' and is used to describe any qualified member of the profession. Once the full training is completed architects are eligible to register with the Architects' Registration Board (ARB); only then are they allowed by law to call themselves an architect. The role of an architect will vary considerably between practices, and according to his/her position within a particular practice. The architect at the head of a practice is usually more of a businessman than a designer, whose primary concerns would be attracting new clients and managing the company. A newly recruited architect might spend his or her first year working on certain detailed aspects of a number of existing projects before progressing on to running his or her own jobs.

Project architect

Most architects will soon reach the stage where they are running their own projects within a practice. The architect who is responsible for the conceptual design, detailed design and project management for a particular building is referred to as the project or job architect.

Once he or she has been assigned to a particular job, the first thing the project architect will have to do is develop a conceptual design which meets the requirements of the client, the characteristics of the site, and which satisfies the local planning authority and any other relevant regulatory bodies (e.g. English Heritage). This conceptual design, or scheme, is presented to the client and to other members of the design team using drawings, sketches, models and, increasingly, computer techniques. Once the scheme has been approved by the client, and planning permission has been gained, the project architect will begin work on the detailed design of the building.

For most buildings, the detailed design is the most time-consuming element of the project architect's work. This involves developing the building design in consultation with other professionals such as the structural engineer and the fire officer, to a stage where a final set of detailed scale drawings can be produced for use on site by the builder. These drawings will also be presented to the quantity surveyor for use in producing the bill of quantities, and to the local authority for Building Regulations approval.

Architectural technologist (technician)

Architects employ architectural technologists (or technicians) to assist them with the detailed design and production of working drawings, and often rely on them to give advice and information about construction principles, specification of materials, etc. Architectural technologists will frequently know considerably more about the 'nuts and bolts' of how a building is put together than the architect does, and it is not uncommon for an architect to pass over the majority of the detailed design to an experienced architectural technologist.

Computer-aided design (CAD) technician

As with just about every other industry, the construction industry – and architecture in particular – has been dramatically affected by the increased widespread use of computers. During the past fifteen years, specialised computer programs for the production of working drawings and three-dimensional images have revolutionised the way in which architects work. Indeed, for many practices the use of computer-aided design (CAD) programs has become so important that many now employ specialist CAD architectural technologists to do this work. The accuracy of the drawings produced, and ease of repetition of standard elements such as doors and windows, make this technique highly desirable for the production of drawings for use on site. Some of the more sophisticated programs offer 'solid modelling' which enable virtual models of the building to be created and viewed from any angle, showing detail such as materials, colour schemes and the effects of natural and artificial lighting, before any building work has begun.

Interior designer

Most architectural projects will require the architect to think about both the external and internal appearances of the new building. However, there will be some projects where, for a variety of possible reasons, the client or architect chooses to appoint a specialist interior designer. Such projects might include an art gallery, concert hall or private house where the client will also be the owner of the building. The interior designer might become involved at an early stage to consult with the architect on matters such as natural lighting, choice of materials and colour schemes. Alternatively, the interior designer may be brought in to look at specialist issues such as furniture, fixtures and fittings after the building has been completed and the architect's work is done.

Landscape architect

One of the primary concerns for any architectural project is to strike a balance between the building that is being created and its natural environment. For buildings in inner city locations, the addition of trees and other plants both inside and around the site can have a dramatic effect on the new development. And for country locations where the new development might occupy a greenfield site, the handling of the natural environment is clearly of paramount importance. It is for this reason that landscape architects are being increasingly used by architects to handle this aspect of their work.

It is the job of the landscape architect to produce the landscape scheme for a building project, presented using drawings and models. Landscape architects are trained in the design of both 'hard' landscaping and 'soft' landscaping. Hard landscaping refers to any non-living building element used around the building, such as paving, brick walls, fencing and seating. Soft landscaping refers to all horticultural elements such as grass, shrubs and trees. Landscape architects are very knowledgeable about the use, durability and weathering properties of different building materials, and the way they interact both physically and chemically with different plant species. They are not purely horticulturists.

Model-maker

One of the problems with two-dimensional line drawings as a means of communicating a three-dimensional design is that the client often finds it difficult to visualise the building and how it will look on its site. It is not uncommon for architects to make rough models as part of the normal design process, either for presentation to the client or simply to help their own understanding of the scheme they are designing. However, on larger projects, or where the budget permits, specialist architectural model-makers may be used. Model-makers produce scale models from the architect's drawings, which can range from simple block models to highly intricate scale replicas of the real building, incorporating appropriate materials, lighting, colour scheme and landscaping. For such projects it is not uncommon for the final model to account for around one per cent of the total cost of the project (models costing £1m or more are not unheard of).

Perspective artist

Another effective option for the architect working on a project where a model-maker would be too expensive is to employ a perspective artist or illustrator. Often trained architects themselves, perspective artists produce full-colour paintings or drawings of the proposed building as it would look after it was built – complete with cars, people, landscaping and surrounding buildings. An advantage of the perspective artist over the model-maker is the speed at which the work is done – in some cases a perspective artist briefed in the morning can have a fully rendered drawing ready by the end of the day.

What qualifications will I need?

The only way to become an architect in the UK is by passing, or gaining exemption from, the following RIBA examinations:

- RIBA Examination in Architecture: Part 1
- RIBA Examination in Architecture: Part 2
- RIBA Professional Practice Examination: Part 3

In the vast majority of cases this is achieved by a combination of full- or part-time study and a minimum period of two years' structured and recorded architectural experience. RIBA Part 1 normally involves studying for a three-year RIBA/ARB-recognised degree course (four years part-time). Part 2 involves completion of the first 'year out' in practice followed by a return to university or college for a two-year diploma (three years part-time). The diploma may be studied at the school where you studied your degree, or elsewhere. Part 3 involves completion of the second year of practical experience, and of the final professional practice examination.

Architect: Full–time study

The majority of entrants to architectural training attend a full-time course at a school of architecture approved by RIBA and ARB. Of the 39 schools currently in the UK, 35 are in universities, two are affiliated to art colleges (the Kent Institute of Art and Design in Canterbury and the Royal College of Art in London) and two are independent (the Architectural Association and the Prince of Wales's Institute of Architecture, both in London).

Below are the latest figures from UCAS for applicants to full-time architecture degree courses at universities in the UK.

	Men	Women	Total
Applied	1,887	1,065	2,952
Accepted	1,641	894	2,535
Success rate	(87%)	(84%)	(86%)

Training to become an architect takes a minimum of seven years full time, and this usually involves five years at university (a three-year degree and a two-year diploma) and two years in professional practice – one year usually taken after the degree (the 'year out') and one after the diploma.

The majority of architects currently entering the architectural profession in this country do so via one of the schools of architecture offering a course recognised by RIBA (a list of recognised courses is given on the RIBA website at www.architecture.com). While entry requirements differ slightly between schools, the following provides a guide to minimum entry requirements as of 2001:

GCSEs, AS- and A-levels

You will normally need at least two academic subjects at A-level, or one A- and two AS-levels. (Applicants should note that in some schools Engineering Drawing A-level is not acceptable.) In addition, you must have passed at least five GCSEs including English Language, Maths and two science subjects. The RIBA recommends that at least three of the GCSE subjects are different to the A-level subjects.

A handful of schools of architecture insist on Maths or a science at A-level, but most are flexible. Generally, all schools are looking for a good mix of science and art subjects at both GCSE and A-level (or equivalent).

The Scottish Certificate of Education

The requirements are similar to the above except that at least 3 of the subjects should be passed on the Ordinary grade. Passes in any 2 of the additional mathematical subjects (Elementary Analysis, Geometry, and Dynamics) will count as 1 Higher grade for this purpose. All 3 Higher grade subjects and 1 Ordinary grade subject should be drawn from the fields of study specified above.

GNVQ/BTEC Qualifications

Students with suitable GNVQ/BTEC Diplomas or Certificates and GCSEs are accepted by most UK schools of architecture. GNVQ/BTEC category candidates are advised to contact schools of architecture.

The University of Cambridge Overseas School and Higher School Certificate

The requirements are similar to the above except that at least 2 of the 5 subjects should be passes as Principal Subjects in the Overseas High School Certificate. The remaining subjects may be passed either with Credit or Distinction in the Overseas School Certificate or as subsidiary subjects in the Overseas Higher School Certificate.

Architect: Part-time study

If you are currently working in an architects' office, you can train to become an architect on a part-time day-release basis. Requirements for part-time students are identical to those for full-time students, and the amount of time needed to study while carrying out a full-time job should not be underestimated. Part-time students typically spend four years gaining RIBA Part 1 (instead of the usual three) and three years instead of two gaining RIBA Part 2.

External entry

In addition to the full- and part-time training routes, RIBA conducts a small number of external examinations at Part 1 and Part 2 levels for candidates who have not completed one of the approved courses of architecture referred to above. These examinations have no formal course of study, but rely on structured work experience and examinations.

Architectural technologist (technician)

For those who have chosen to make architectural technology their career, you have to work towards full membership of the British Institute of Architectural Technologists (BIAT). To do this, the most relevant subjects to study at GCSE are Maths, science (double or triple is best), design and technology, information technology and English. Art is also a useful option.

After GCSE there are a number of choices. For example, you may take:

- A/AS-levels in science and technology subjects
- BTEC National Certificate/Diploma in building studies
- GNVQ (Advanced) in the built environment

followed by:

- A degree in architectural technology or related subject
- An NVQ/SVQ level 4 in architectural technology
- A Higher National Certificate/Diploma in architectural design (with additional units).

At this point you will be eligible to apply for associate membership of BIAT, where you will be able to use the letters ABIAT after your name. This demonstrates your commitment to gaining professional status and recognises that you have completed the academic stage of your training.

To become a full member you must complete a further round of assessments against professional standards, including submission of a two to three year supervised BIAT work diary and attendance at a professional assessment interview. Information on courses and a career in architectural technology can be found in the BIAT publication *Your Career As An Architectural Technologist*.

BIAT operates a network of 15 regional centres within the UK through which student members can get involved with the professional community, establish contacts, gain an insight into the opportunities open to them, and learn from the technical expertise of qualified members.

What personal skills and attitudes are needed?

Architect

All buildings are the product of compromise. The number of contributory factors which affect the design and production of even the smallest project have rendered this inevitable. As society becomes more complex and technology advances, so the compromise becomes greater.

One of the most important qualities a modern architect can possess is therefore the ability to juggle the requirements of the different professionals involved on the project through to a mutually satisfactory conclusion without any dilution of the original design concept. In short, an architect must be both visionary and diplomatic.

Other key skills for an architect are as follows:

Communication skills – the effective communication of ideas, knowledge and opinions is central to an architect's work. The ability to express ideas visually through sketches, drawings or models, as well as through the spoken and written word, is therefore essential.

Problem-solving – much of an architect's work concerns finding practical, elegant solutions to the various problems thrown up by the project. Architects tend to view problems as challenges or opportunities, aiming to solve them in as lateral and creative a way as possible. This approach can often make all the difference to the finished building.

Diplomacy – the requirements of other professionals working on a project, not to mention those of the client, can often seem completely at odds with what the architect wants to achieve and believes to be right. Sensitive handling of such situations is therefore an important skill.

Art/science balance – one of the struggles continuously faced by architects is the tempering of a design concept by practicalities of structure and planning. A good architect therefore needs to be able to balance the practical and logical with the artistic and creative.

Sensitivity – architects create the spaces and places in which others live, work and relax. Because what they do is so visible, it is important that architects are sensitive towards the environment, the public viewpoint, the clients' requirements, and other professionals' requirements, so that their work offends as few people as possible.

Management skills – as head of the design team, the architect has to be a good manager both of his own staff and of other professionals. As you progress through your career as an architect, the amount of management and administration work you do is likely to outweigh the design work, and therefore good time management skills are also crucial.

Numeracy – a high level of numeracy is very important when working as an architect, and many schools still stipulate A-level Maths as an entry requirement. Everyday work such as producing scale drawings, surveying existing buildings and sites, and calculating the insulation properties of a composite wall all require basic numeracy. More complex mathematics are involved when designing the structure of the building (in short, whether or not it will stand up), and, although this is the structural engineer's job, the architect has to have a working knowledge of structure in order to discuss the building in the engineer's terms.

Robustness and flexibility – when you have worked hard to come up with a good design which you believe to be right, it is not always easy to accept alterations. However, issues such as the clients' lack of money or vision; last-minute changes in the brief;

planning, legal, fire or conservation regulations; and structural alterations can all lead to major changes and sometimes even to the termination of a project. As with all creative subjects, architects can become protective about their work, but this should not be allowed to obstruct the right course of action.

Commitment – in many ways the seven years of architectural training acts as its own filter for the uncommitted. It is a long, tough course and in most schools the architects' studio lights burn through the night. This, however, is necessary preparation for work within the profession. Most architects' practices are small, and most small practices will require a certain number of late nights and weekends to be worked without paying overtime, in order to meet deadlines.

Creativity – it sounds obvious, but if you are not a naturally creative person you probably will not make a good architect. Several schools list A-level Art as a preference, and all schools will want to see a portfolio of art work before places are awarded.

Natural ability to make or mend things – much of what an architect does concerns understanding how things are put together, and how to convert two-dimensional drawings into three-dimensional objects. If you are interested in making things, mending things or simply dismantling things then you will already have acquired some of the skills needed to become a good architect.

Architectural technologist (technician)

It is the architectural technologist's job to turn the architect's concept into a reality, and a good architectural technologist will therefore act as a practical foil to the architect's creativity. While many of the skills and attributes listed above are crucial for architectural technologists, the following are also important:

Attention to detail – all drawings and models are produced to scale and a high degree of accuracy is necessary to ensure that everything fits when scaled up to life size on site.

Lateral thinking – the architectural technologist will often have to think laterally about the design itself, and in particular the consequences of any changes made. A simple example would be where the client looks at the plan and decides an extra window is needed to provide more natural light. The architectural technologist then has to see how the new window looks from the outside, assess the structural implications, check whether the new window affects the fire or planning regulations, and many other knock-on effects.

Problem-solving – when producing the detailed 'working drawings' for a building from the architect's design drawings, many problems will be thrown up. While working closely with the architect during this phase of the design, a good architectural technologist will have to be as inventive and creative as possible in solving these problems to avoid making unnecessary changes to the design itself.

How competitive
an area is it?

I n March 2000 unemployment among architects in the UK was estimated at just 1%, although this should be viewed in the context of a healthy construction industry – the figure would be higher in times of economic recession. Some areas of architectural work are more difficult to get into than others. If you want to work for Richard Rogers or Norman Foster, you'll have to join a long queue and be able to demonstrate that you are exceptionally good when you get to the front.

Other issues to consider are:

- **Regionality** – the likelihood of getting a job within the architectural profession increases with regional population density. 44% of the architectural profession is based in London and the South East, and in 1999 London alone represented 36% of total earnings for the sector
- **Gender** – only 12% of architects are women, although this situation is improving all the time, with women representing 36% of architectural students in 2000
- **Race** – ethnic minorities are also under-represented within the sector. To help combat this, the RIBA is backing a series of initiatives, for example Architects for Change, to encourage children from diverse backgrounds to engage in their built environment and consider careers in the architectural profession
- **Specialisation** – if you are passionate about working on a particular type of building or building style then you are narrowing your options considerably and are likely to find it harder to find work that meets your specific requirements.

What are the good and bad aspects of the work?

Pros

The most rewarding aspect of an architect's work must be the sheer job satisfaction: few careers can offer the sense of achievement which comes from seeing your designs converted into full-scale buildings in which people live, work and enjoy themselves. Many young architects find that a high level of responsibility comes quite quickly after qualification and many architects feel able to set up their own business comparatively early in their career. The skills gained as an architect will also enable you to do what you want with your own house.

Cons

The building industry is very sensitive to changes in the economy, and is always hit hard by recession. Architects are very much beholden to their clients and to the various regulatory authorities. Design concepts are nearly always watered down and every finished building is a compromise. On large projects within large practices it is possible for newly qualified architects to get stuck on the details of the building and to lose track of the overall concept of the project, and of the developments within the profession itself. You will also invariably find that as you progress within the profession, the ratio of design to management changes in favour of management.

Where will I work?

The following table shows UK architects practice size by number of architectural staff:

1 architectural staff	18%
2 architectural staff	12%
3–5 architectural staff	16%
6–10 architectural staff	15%
11–30 architectural staff	20%
31–50 architectural staff	8%
50+ architectural staff	11%

(Source: *Architects Employment and Earnings*, RIBA 2000)

It can be seen from these statistics that most architects currently employed in the UK (81%) work in companies with 30 or fewer employees, and nearly half in practices with fewer than 6 staff. One question often asked of architects is 'What is your area of specialisation?' The fact is, however, that most architects' practices do not operate within a particular specialist area. Architectural training equips the student with the skills to take on just about any project. Thus the main factor governing the type of work undertaken by a particular practice is the size, or contract value, of the project. The higher the contract value, the fewer projects there will be, and the fewer practices there will be with sufficient staffing and resources to undertake the work.

Private practice

In 2000 there were 20,900 architects in full-time employment in the UK, the vast majority of which (79%) worked in one of the UK's 6,000 private practices. The remaining 21% were split into public sector architects (15%) and those working outside the construction industry altogether (6%).

Private practices range in size from the one-man band running a handful of small local projects to the large international firm with several offices spread over more than one country and with hundreds of employees.

As creators of the internal spaces and environments in which people live, work and relax, you will often find when visiting an architect's own office that they have designed, converted or re-modelled the space in which they work. Architects' offices are therefore as much about providing accommodation fit for the business of designing buildings, as about creating a space which promotes their particular style and skills to potential clients.

Multidisciplinary companies

There are also a number of firms in which architects, engineers, surveyors and other building professionals work together under the same roof. These 'multidisciplinary' companies are generally larger than architects' firms, and have several advantages: they facilitate cross-fertilisation between the different disciplines e.g. clients looking for a surveyor can also be offered an architectural service; they avoid doubling up on secretarial and other support staff/services; and they avoid the need to approach outside companies when putting together the design team for each job. However, such companies are fairly inflexible, carry large overheads and can be more vulnerable during a recession.

Public sector

There has been a steady decline during recent years in the number of architects working in the public sector. Many central government divisions have now been privatised, such as the Property Services Agency. In addition, local authority architects' departments, although not privatised, are now required to compete with private architects for much of the work which previously would have been given to the department automatically. Although this has led to a more competitive arena where borough and county architects' offices are able to compete for work both in their immediate area and beyond, it has also led to a decline in the amount of work undertaken by local authority architects' departments.

However, 15% of all architects are still employed by the public sector. The main strength of public sector work is that, unlike many private practices, public sector architects do have a specific area of expertise, which makes them very competitive in their niche. The downside of this is that the work is often regarded as less exciting than private practice.

The work undertaken by a local authority architects' department would be primarily council-owned buildings such as courthouses, doctors' surgeries, leisure facilities, old peoples' homes, police buildings, schools and village halls. A typical office might contain between five and ten architects and anywhere between five and 15 architectural technologists, but, again, this is decreasing.

Who will I work with?

The client

The client is the person or body who commissions the building. This can range from an individual commissioning a private house or extension to an organisation such as a company, local authority or charity. It is normally only the senior architects within a practice who deal with the client, although the level of involvement a client has with the design team during the design of the building will vary.

The design team

The design team has already been mentioned several times. This is the team of architects, architectural technologists and specialists (such as structural engineer, services engineers and quantity surveyor) who produce the building design under the direction of the project architect. Working as an architect you will spend much of your time as part of, or in charge of, a design team.

Builders

The architect will spend much of his or her time on site during the construction stages of a building. During this time it is important to try and develop a working knowledge of the large number of skilled crafts involved in producing a new building. Architects need to be able to deal with bricklayers, carpenters, electricians, plasterers, etc., using the correct terminology involved with these different skills.

Regulatory authorities

At roughly the same time as the builders are invited to tender, a set of drawings is also sent to the various regulatory authorities for their approval. All building work must be given both Building Regulations approval and planning permission by the local council. In addition, once Building Regulations approval has been granted, a Building Inspector from the local authority will make inspections on site at various stages during the building's construction to ensure that the work is being carried out satisfactorily. It is also necessary for most projects to consult with specially trained fire officers either at the local fire station, or at fire service headquarters.

What will I earn?

Compared with most other professions involving a similar duration of formal training, architecture is not particularly well paid.

The following table gives an approximate guide to the average annual salaries architects and architectural technologists can expect, although – as with any profession – the salaries vary enormously according to factors such as experience, location, type of practice, particular area of specialisation, etc:

Architects

Post first degree/Part 1 'year out' students:	£13,000–17,000
Recent post-diploma/Part 2/ pre-Part 3 assistants:	£20,000–24,000
Newly registered architects/ 0–3 years post-Part 3:	£23,000–27,000
Job architects with 3–5 years post-Part 3 experience:	£26,000–32,000

Beyond this point salary expectation will depend considerably upon the particular firm and job, but a very general guide for architects aged 30-plus would be:

Job architect with a small firm:	£25,000–28,000
Job architect with a larger/commercial firm:	£28,000–32,000
Team leader with a larger/commercial firm:	£30,000–35,000
Associate with a small firm:	£28,000–34,000
Associate with a larger/ commercial firm:	£32,000–38,000

(Source: RIBA)

Architectural technologists

Senior (CAD proficient)	£28,500–37,000
Junior	£15,000–19,500

(Source: www.architects-online.org)

When looking at these figures, the following general points should be noted:

- Candidates with CAD skills can almost invariably command figures at the upper end of the quoted ranges; the most sought after CAD skills are Autocad, Microstation and Minicad
- There is variation from region to region and from practice to practice. London (where 28% of the profession is based) pays more than the rest of the country
- Large firms generally pay more than small ones, with commercial and industrial firms paying the most
- For a young architect the quality and variety of work undertaken during the first few years are every bit as important as the salary, and in many cases some of the less well-paid jobs will provide a much broader experience and higher level of responsibility than those with the more attractive salaries.

The RIBA publishes an annual salary survey, the main aspects of which are published in the RIBA Journal each summer.

What are the hours and holidays like?

A rchitects are often required to work long hours, perhaps finishing drawings for a presentation to a client or getting a competition entry ready to meet the deadline. The frequency of such long hours will depend very much on the specific workload and scheduling of the firm concerned, but the ethic of working late will by this time have long been ingrained into your way of life from your college days where staying up late (and sometimes all night) in the design studio to finish projects is the norm rather than the exception.

For architects working in the UK, the average holiday entitlement is 23 days per annum, which corresponds with the normal entitlement of 20 days for a new job, increasing after a certain number of years (usually five) by one day a year.

Will I meet the public?

G enerally speaking, no. Architects are employed by a client to produce a building, which they do in consultation with various other professionals. Most of the work is done either in the office or on site. However, during those parts of the work which are carried out outside, such as site visits and surveys, architects will inevitably have a small amount of contact with the public.

There might also be occasions where the architect is required to speak at a town, city or county council meeting in order to argue the case for a new building on behalf of his or her client. This would usually only occur where an objection had been made, and such situations can often lead to confrontation with the public.

In addition, there could be certain special occasions where an architect might meet the public: a particular building or development might win an award for which there would be a presentation ceremony; alternatively, a prestigious building might be officially opened by a celebrity or dignitary.

Finally, if you become famous or notorious, even at a local level, you might well be asked to make various after-dinner speeches, and give seminars and lectures.

Are the prospects good for my career?

G enerally speaking, yes. After a long and demanding qualification period you will be eligible to register with the ARB, join one of the professional architectural institutions such as RIBA and enter a well-established industry, for which there will always be a demand. Moving between jobs and entering new areas of specialisation are comparatively easy to do, and since the majority of architectural practices is small, many architects are able to set up on their own soon after joining the profession. In addition, UK architectural qualifications are accepted around the world, so a move to another country should be comparatively easy.

However, while unemployment within the sector currently stands at around 1%, the effects of changes in the national economy on the building industry can be dramatic, and with a seven-year training period it would be possible to begin your qualification during a boom, and to qualify during a recession and find that there is no work.

Architecture and the building industry itself are also constantly developing to reflect changes in the social, political and technological environment which surrounds them. As with any profession, such developments will generate the need for new areas of expertise, as well as spell the end for some of the older ones. Architects must therefore remain sensitive to changes occurring within the broader profession and ensure that they equip themselves with appropriate skills to keep up.

What about training at work?

As has been mentioned before, a minimum of two years' practical experience working in an office is required in order to qualify as an architect or as an architectural technologist. It should also be stressed that with architecture, possibly more than any other profession, the real learning process does not begin until you are in your first job producing live working drawings, sorting out problems on site and dealing day to day with the other professionals in the field. It can come as a shock having done seven years training to discover, when you begin your first job, that an 18-year-old apprentice technician knows far more about the practical aspects of building than a newly qualified architect.

Architect

If you are currently working in an architect's office, you can train to become an architect on a part-time basis (see p. 12).

RIBA has also recently devised a special route to qualification for students with extensive practical experience, but with no formal architectural qualifications, which puts emphasis on practical knowledge, with fewer examinations and projects. RIBA puts an upper limit on the number of students taking this route each year, as each applicant has to be assessed individually to determine the level of experience gained.

Architectural technologist

A special BIAT qualification route exists (Route 3) specifically for applicants aged 30 years and over with at least ten years' relevant experience and with or without formal qualifications.

Will I need other languages for the work?

Y ou will not normally need to speak another language in order to progress and be successful as an architect in the UK. However, as Britain becomes increasingly involved with the rest of Europe, many architectural practices will be seeking work abroad, in the same way that many European architects will be looking to expand their business into the UK.

Furthermore, significant international markets exist for British architects in the US and countries in the Pacific Rim: Japan, Hong Kong, Malaysia and South Korea.

Obviously in this situation fluency in, or even a working knowledge of, a language other than English would be a clear advantage, even though much international business is conducted in English. Practices with a particular area of expertise might become involved in work in any number of non-English speaking countries. For instance, a company specialising in the design of concert halls and auditoria might find that only a handful of such buildings are commissioned each year throughout the world. A second language when working for a company with this level of specialisation could therefore lead to a high level of involvement in some very exciting projects in countries where that language was spoken.

Will I be able to work overseas or travel for my job?

Overseas travel

British architects are well known for the aesthetic quality and forward-looking nature of their design. There are many British flagship projects in the US, the Far East and Europe, including the highly acclaimed new German Parliament built within the walls of Berlin's former Reichstag by Foster and Partners.

A position in one of the larger architectural firms could bring with it opportunities to travel and work almost anywhere in the world. Similarly, as Britain develops closer links with the rest of the EU, an increasing number of smaller practices are also looking for work overseas.

It is estimated that in 2000 around 3,800 British architects were working abroad, a rise of 80% on the 1998 figure of 2,100; the most important destinations are the EU, British Commonwealth nations, and the US. However, overseas travel cannot be guaranteed, since many practices will have enough work within the UK.

Domestic travel

Travel within the UK is more often than not an intrinsic part of any architect's work. It would be usual for even the smallest firms to be running simultaneous jobs in a number of different areas, and since no architectural project can be managed entirely from the office, architects often have to travel over a wide area in order to attend regular site visits.

What are the recent developments in this area?

A rchitecture and the building industry itself are constantly developing to reflect changes in the social, political and technological environment which surrounds them. Here are a few of the recent developments.

Information technology

Developments in IT are beginning to transform the way in which the modern architect works. CAD software has largely eliminated the traditional pen and ink drawings, and 3-d modelling software enables architects to create and explore virtual buildings before a brick has been laid.

In the near future architects are likely to be required to produce web pages to accompany their building designs to enable clients and suppliers to view the scheme remotely, and enable property developers and real estate agents to sell it.

But at present digital services are inconsistently employed across the construction sector. This is most likely to be the result of concern over the inefficiencies of new systems (e.g. software still at the development stage, slow download speeds) and the need to develop more familiarity with and confidence in the opportunities technology can generate.

The training of architects in future should accommodate these evolving requirements.

Intelligent materials

Developments in materials science and knowledge have always been reflected in the buildings around us. But research into 'intelligent materials' – which involves ways to manipulate atoms and molecules into desired configurations – may soon herald truly monumental changes in architecture. Consider some of the possibilities:

- Shape-memory alloys that can return to their original shape after having been stressed
- Piezo-electric materials that expand and contract in response to an applied voltage
- Magneto-strictive materials that re-shape in response to magnetic fields
- Electro-rheological and magneto-rheological fluids that change viscosity in response to electrical and magnetic fields
- Smart materials with embedded sensors that deliver light, sound, information, or messages to and from each other
- Self-assembling materials, like organic cells, that can create exact replicas of themselves.

The effects of introducing these technologies into architecture could turn traditional architectural vocabularies on their head. Walls could cease to be solid structures and instead become sheets of colour, sound, and images. Balconies or roofs could stretch out or shrink in depending on the sun. A building might recoil under the adverse conditions of too much noise or illumination. Buildings could even undertake their own repairs or environmental audits.

It might sound like science fiction, but many of these materials are already beginning to be used in the aerospace and engineering industries.

Energy

Dwindling supplies of fossil fuels have led to a heightened awareness of the importance of conserving energy. The UK Building Regulations specify minimum insulation levels for all external building elements (including floors), and in some

Scandinavian countries the development of technologies such as argon-filled triple-glazing and super insulation have led to the creation of houses in which the occupiers hardly ever need to switch on the heating.

Environment

Awareness of the importance of the natural environment is currently at an all-time high. It is therefore very important that today's architects are sensitive in their designs and think carefully about the use of materials, natural light, methods of waste disposal and landscaping.

What impact has new technology had on this work?

The technological advances which have been made within the IT industry over the past two decades have had a dramatic impact on the architectural profession.

By 2003 the construction industry expects to handle 10% of its £56 billion output via the Internet. At present, e-commerce is employed mainly for ordering building products, but in the near future it is envisaged that it will enable companies to network the participants of construction projects – clients, contractors, professionals, tradesmen and suppliers – more effectively.

In addition, drawing and 3-d modelling CAD software packages have largely eradicated the old method of pen and ink drawings on tracing paper. The majority of schools of architecture now have state-of-the-art CAD systems, and much of the coursework is now being done on computer rather than at the drawing board.

Could I become famous?

It is more likely that one of your buildings will achieve either fame or notoriety than that you yourself will become a household name. Thus the Millennium Wheel, the Sydney Opera House and the Houses of Parliament are all more famous than their respective architects David Marks, Jorn Utson and Sir Charles Barry. (One notable exception might be St Paul's Cathedral whose architect Sir Christopher Wren is as famous as his buildings!)

However, a general increase in awareness of architecture and the built environment, famously championed by Prince Charles, has led to the emergence of a number of modern-day architecture personalities and political figures, chief among them:

- Lord (Richard) Rogers (The Millennium Dome and Lloyd's Building in London and the Pompidou Centre in Paris, with Renzo Piano), famous for putting all the innards of his buildings on the outside, and for his plans for central London which include the pedestrianisation of Trafalgar Square and the Embankment
- Sir Norman Foster (London Millennium Bridge (with engineering firm Arup), Hong Kong and Shanghai Bank in Hong Kong, and Wembley Stadium Masterplan), famous for being the pioneer of high-tech architecture.

The chances of becoming this well-known on the international architecture scene are extremely slim. But each of these architects, and other famous names both here and abroad, run large practices, often with offices in various countries, and if you are good enough, and more specifically if your designs are in the right style, you might well be able to get a job with one of the stars.

Could I work independently?

A t one level, yes. Most architectural practices employ fewer than ten people, and 30% of those in the UK employ only one or two architects. Obviously many architects are setting up on their own, or with a partner, and are being successful. However, doing this will inevitably bring restrictions to the type and size of projects which you are able to handle. Most one- or two-man band practices will be carrying out work up to a maximum project value of around £1m. This could include, for example, one-off houses, small schools and libraries, etc., and all kinds of renovation work. Airports, hospitals, large office or shopping complexes, auditoria and stadiums would all be far too large to handle.

Possibly the greatest independence is to be gained by working as a self-employed architect, architectural technologist or surveyor on a freelance basis. By contracting your services out to other companies you will have total control over the amount and type of work you do, though of course you will always have to work to your client's budget and deadlines.

However, at another level, it is not possible for an architect to work independently. An architect's work necessarily involves interaction with a large number of outside professionals and services, without whom no building project would ever get off the ground. This, therefore, is definitely not the profession for a reclusive type who does not like getting out and meeting people.

How can I find out more about the work?

Architecture centres and galleries

There is a network of architectural organisations throughout the country who provide information, events and exhibitions on architecture (contact details given at the back of this book).

Architecture Week

Over 400 events around the country provide people a chance to learn more about architecture, buildings and spaces. Events include Open Practice, an opportunity to visit architects in their offices and ask questions. Contact the RIBA for further details.

Exhibitions/museums

A good way for prospective architects to learn more about the profession is to attend one of the wide variety of architectural exhibitions, degree shows or museums around the UK. Exhibitions are frequently mounted (especially in London) in order to give leading contemporary architects from all over the world the chance to display drawings, models and photographs of their latest projects. A number of permanent exhibitions and museums also exist, frequently within famous buildings themselves, such as the Lloyd's Building exhibition (4th floor, Lloyd's Building, London). Among the other architectural museums worth visiting are the Sir John Soane Museum in Lincoln's Inn Fields, London, and the Weald and Downland Museum in West Sussex. In addition, there is a network of architectural organisations throughout the country who provide information, events and exhibitions on architecture, and these are listed on pages 49–52.

You should also be aware that university and college architecture departments generally mount degree and diploma shows during June/July where members of the public are invited to view the work of the student architects. This is an excellent way for anyone considering entering architecture school to see the type and standard of the work they will be expected to produce.

Internet

As with everything else, there is an almost infinite amount of information relating to architecture on the Internet, and the difficulty is finding the best sites. The RIBA site www.architecture.com is a good starting point, as is their portal site at www.riba.org/library/rlinks/htm. For those who are serious about becoming an architect the ARB site provides all the formal stuff at www.arb.org.uk/frame.html, and the RIBA annual medal competition entries plus other useful info can be seen at www.presidentsmedals.com.

All the architecture schools have sites which are worth looking at and many of the larger practices in the UK also have sites where you can look at the work they have done.

Books, journals and newspapers

The range of published material covering all aspects of architecture is so vast that it is often difficult for a prospective student architect to know what to read (see p. 46 for some suggestions). Try choosing a book on a specific architect whose name you know, or whose work you like the look of from the cover. A quick look through some indexes might show that there are buildings by some well-known architects in your area which you could go and have a look at.

You will also find that most quality newspapers have an architecture section or feature which offers a cheaper way of keeping abreast of the industry.

Television programmes

All the benefits normally associated with television make this an excellent medium through which to learn about architects and their buildings. During recent years there has been a number of excellent television series and one-off documentaries covering the work of different architects (contemporary and historic) or addressing a range of architectural issues. Many of these will be available on video from the architectural library once you get into university or college.

What should I do now to prepare?

General

In the period leading up to your application to architecture school, try to find out as much as you can about the profession and about buildings themselves. Visit your school or college careers library to research the various courses and options. Read the daily newspapers (many have an architecture section) and have a look at the main trade journals (see page 46) and websites.

Perhaps most importantly of all, try to develop an awareness of the buildings you are in and around from day to day. When do you think your house or school were built? How are the ceilings, window openings and staircases supported? How might the building have been assembled and what is it made of? How much extra would the roof weigh if it was covered in snow? You don't actually have to know or even find out the answers to any of these questions – but you should get into the habit of asking them.

You might also consider visiting the local town hall and looking at some pending planning applications. Try also to take notice of the buildings you walk past, through, underneath or over. And remember that building sites will become your second home, so don't just walk past them like everyone else does, but have a good look – you will learn a lot about basic construction techniques if you do.

Portfolio

The ability to communicate ideas through drawings and sketches is central to an architect's work, and all schools of architecture will ask you to show a portfolio of work demonstrating your ability in this area. Do not underestimate the amount of time it will take to prepare your portfolio. GCSE and A-level art students will be able to include much of their coursework, but remember you are applying for a course in architecture and it is therefore advisable that your portfolio contains some drawings, sketches, models or photographs of buildings. Technical drawing skills are not necessary at this stage as these will be learnt at architecture school.

Some colleges of further education run summer holiday courses to help you build up a portfolio of work – particularly useful if you're not studying A-level Art.

Work experience

While work experience before the beginning of an architectural course is not a requirement, it would undoubtedly be useful in helping you decide whether you enjoy and are suited to the work, and would go down well with admissions tutors. No amount of reading or study can replace hands-on experience and contact with professionals actually doing the job.

Some architects will take school students for one or two weeks' work experience – usually at Year 10 and Year 12 – to help with career and university course choices. If work experience is not possible, a short interview with a practising architect would give you some useful insights, and might also prove useful when looking for a 'year out' placement after your degree.

Work experience need not necessarily be in an architects' office. For example, you will learn a tremendous amount by labouring on a building site, or perhaps assisting your parents or a friend or colleague with any building work they might be doing – even if it's only erecting a garden shed or greenhouse.

If no work experience is available, you could try simply measuring a building (e.g. your house) and then drawing plans and elevations to scale. This kind of initiative could make all the difference on the UCAS form or in an interview.

Degree shows

All schools of architecture run end-of-year degree shows at which Part 1 and Part 2 final year students' work is shown. One of the best ways to see if architecture is for you is to attend the degree show at your nearest school. And, once inside a school of architecture, you might be given the opportunity to have a look around too.

What courses and qualifications are available?

You may well by now have decided that you want to work/study in the construction industry but are still not sure which discipline to pursue. The range of post-16 courses and qualifications available for those wishing to enter the construction industry is enormous. It is therefore important that anyone wishing to enter one of the construction disciplines sets some time aside to research the types of course available – even if you think you know exactly what you want to do.

Detailed careers and educational information including lists of accredited courses for prospective architects is given on the RIBA website at www.architecture.com. Aspiring architectural technologists should consult the BIAT website at www.biat.org.uk.

Once you have decided what you want to do, detailed course information is available on the UCAS website at www.ucas.ac.uk.

What publications should I look at?

Periodicals

Architects Journal (weekly)

Architectural Review (monthly)

Building Design (weekly)

RIBA Journal (monthly)

Architectural Technology (bi-monthly)

Books

Working In Construction (COIC)

Working In Buildings and Property (COIC)

Careers In Architecture (Kogan Page Limited)

Careers and Courses in the Construction Industry (Construction Industry Training Board (CITB))

Art & Design Courses (Trotman)

Degree Course Offers (Trotman)

Modern Architecture since 1900, William J. R. Curtis (Phaidon Press Limited)

Architecture For Beginners, Louis Hellman (Writers and Readers Publishing Cooperative (Unwin))

Architecture: Form, Space and Order, Francis D.K. Ching (Van Nostrand Reinhold Company, Inc.)

A History Of Architecture, Sir Banister Fletcher (Athlone Press)

Leaflets

A Career In Architecture – available from any branch of RIBA

Your Career as an Architectural Technologist – available from BIAT

Which addresses will help me?

Whichever construction industry discipline or profession you are considering, one of the best places to start looking for information is the relevant professional body. Prospective architects should contact RIBA, either at the central office or at one of the regional branches, and those looking for a career in architectural technology should contact BIAT.

High quality careers information relating to the industry as a whole, with special emphasis on working for construction companies, can be obtained from the Construction Industry Training Board (CITB).

For professional advice on the most appropriate course or career, contact your local careers service company, who will be able to help you decide which career is best for you, pinpoint your specific needs and point you in the right direction for further information.

Finally, the best way to find out more about a specific course is to contact the department running the course directly. You might be able to find out what you want over the phone or in a letter. Alternatively, all architecture schools have open days or exhibition times where you will be able to go and look round.

Architects and Surveyors Institute (ASI)
St Mary House,
15 St Mary Street,
Chippenham, Wiltshire,
SN15 3WD
Tel: 01249 444 505
Fax: 01249 443 602
Email: asi@asi.org.uk
Website: www.asi.org.uk

Architects' Registration Board (ARB)
8 Weymouth Street,
London W1N 5BU
Tel: 020 7580 5861
Fax: 020 7436 5269
Email: info@arb.org.uk
Website: www.arb.org.uk

British Institute of Architectural Technologists (BIAT)
397 City Road,
London EC1V 1NH
Tel: 020 7278 2206 or
0800 731 5471
Fax: 020 7837 3194
Email: careers@biat.org.uk
Website: www.biat.org.uk

Construction Industry Training Board (CITB)
Head Office,
Bircham Newton, King's Lynn
Norfolk PE31 6RH
Tel: 01485 577577
Fax: 01485 577497
Email: resource@citb.org.uk
Website: www.citb.co.uk

Royal Institute of British Architects (RIBA)
66 Portland Place,
London W1B 1AD
Tel: 020 7580 5533
Fax: 020 7255 1541
Email: bal@inst.riba.org
Website: www.architecture.com

RIBA REGIONAL OFFICES

RIBA Eastern
The Studio,
High Green,
Great Shelford,
Cambridge CB2 5EG
Tel: 01223 566 285
Fax: 01223 505 142

RIBA East Midlands
4 St. James's Terrace,
Nottingham NG1 6FW
Tel: 0115 941 3650
Fax: 0115 950 7249

RIBA London
66 Portland Place,
London W1N 4AD
Tel: 020 7307 3688
Fax: 020 7307 3788

RIBA North
Floor C, Milburn House,
Dean Street,
Newcastle upon Tyne
NE1 1LE
Tel: 0191 232 4436
Fax: 0191 230 5127

RIBA North West
44–6 King Street,
Knutsford,
Cheshire WA16 6HJ
Tel: 01565 652 927
Fax: 01565 633 732

RIBA South
Sherwood House,
8 Upper High Street,
Winchester,
Hants SO23 8UL
Tel: 01962 878 476
Fax: 01962 878 478

RIBA South East
17 Upper Grosvenor Road,
Tunbridge Wells,
Kent TN1 2DU
Tel: 01892 515 878;
Fax: 01892 513 865

RIBA South West
School of Architecture,
University of Plymouth,
161 Notte Street,
Plymouth PL1 2AR
Tel: 01752 265 921/265 927
Fax: 01752 663 747

RIBA West Midlands
Birmingham & Midlands
Institute, Margaret Street,
Birmingham B3 3SP
Tel: 0121 233 2321
Fax: 0121 233 4946

RIBA Wessex
The Architecture Centre,
Narrow Quay,
Bristol BS1 4QA
Tel: 0117 934 9966
Fax: 0117 934 9391

RIBA Yorkshire
8 Woodhouse Square,
Leeds,
West Yorkshire LS3 1AD
Tel: 0113 245 6250
Fax: 0113 242 6791

**RIBA Wales (Royal Society of
Architects in Wales, RSAW)**
Bute Building,
King Edward VII Avenue,
Cathays Park,
Cardiff CF10 3NB
Tel: 029 20874753/4
Fax: 029 20874 926

**Royal Incorporation Of
Architects In Scotland (RIAS)**
15 Rutland Square,
Edinburgh EH1 2BE
Tel: 0131 229 7545
Fax: 0131 228 2188

**Royal Society Of Ulster
Architects (RSUA)**
2 Mount Charles,
Belfast BT7 1NZ
Tel: 028 9032 3760
Fax: 028 9023 7313

ARCHITECTURE CENTRES AND GALLERIES

There is a network of architectural organisations throughout the country who provide information, events and exhibitions on architecture:

London

RIBA Architecture Gallery

66 Portland Place,
London W1B 1AD
Tel: 020 7580 5533
Fax: 020 7307 3703

The Building Exploratory

Professional Development Centre, Albion Drive,
London E8 4ET
Tel: 020 7275 8555
Fax: 020 7275 9184
Email: mail@building exploratory.org.uk
Website: www.building exploratory.org.uk

The Architecture Foundation

30 Bury Street,
London SW1Y 6AU
Tel/Fax: 020 7839 9380
Email: gallery@architecture foundation.org.uk
Website: www.architecture foundation.org.uk

North West

CUBE

113–15 Portland Street,
Manchester M1 6FB
Tel: 0161 237 5525
Fax: 0161 236 5815
Email: info@cube.org.uk
Website : www.cube.org.uk

Liverpool Architecture and Design Trust

16 Vernon Street,
Liverpool L2 2AY
Tel: 0151 233 4079
Fax: 0151 233 4091
Email: info@ladt.org.uk
Website : www.ladt.org.uk

Scotland

The Lighthouse

11 Mitchell Lane,
Glasgow G1 3NN
Tel: 0141 221 6362
Fax: 0141 221 6395
Email: enquiries@thelighthouse.co.uk
Website : www.thelighthouse.co.uk

North East and Yorkshire

Northern Architecture

Blackfriars, Monk Street,
Newcastle NE1
Tel: 0191 260 2191

South East

Lumley Architects
c/o RIBA Eastern,
The Studio,
High Green, Shelford,
Cambridge CB2 5EG
Tel: 01223 566 285
Fax: 01223 505 142

**North Kent Architecture
Centre**
Chatham Historic Dockyard,
Chatham ME4 4TZ
Tel: 01634 401 166
Fax: 01634 403 302
Email:
info@kentarchitecture.co.uk
Website:
www.architecturecentre.org

South West

The Architecture Centre
Narrow Quay,
Bristol BS1 4QA
Tel: 01179 221 540
Fax: 01179 221 541
Email:
architecturecentre@ukgateway.
net
Website: www.arch-
centre.demon.uk